The Glory Topical Bible

John Eckhardt

ISBN:10: 1522765891
ISBN-13: 978-1522765899

DEDICATION

To all that desire to be filled with Daddy God's Glory in their lives and see it engulf the whole earth.

ACKNOWLEDGMENTS

Special Thanks to Prophet Lauro Adame for contributing to the Greek and Hebrew word list, his commentary, and helping me on this Topical Bible.

INTRODUCTION

Glory is a major theme in the scriptures. God is a God of Glory. The Father is the Father of Glory. The Son is the Lord of Glory. The Holy Spirit is the Spirit of Glory. (Ephesians 1:17, Romans 6:4, John 1:14, 1 Peter 4:14)

It was always the plan of God for the earth to be filled with His Glory. (Numbers 14:21) Through out all ages, His church is a Glorious church. (Ephesians 3:21)

This Topical Bible will help you see how prevalent the theme of Glory is in the scriptures. A revelation of the Glory of God will help you live and operate in the Glory realm. There are certain blessings that are connected to the GLORY. We should have a knowledge of the Glory of the LORD.

The following list of Greek and Hebrew words that are part of the lexicon of the GLORY.

The Hebrew word for GLORY(Exodus 33:18) is KABOD meaning weight, abundance, honor, glory, splendor, wealth, honor, riches, reverence, dignity.

Though there are other Hebrew words that are translated "glory," KABOD is used most often, 200 times.

The Greek word for GLORY is DOXA (Matthew 19:28) meaning honor, renown; glory, an especially divine quality, the unspoken manifestation of God, splendor.

An excerpt from his book called *The Open Door of Glory"* Lauro Adame wrote the following about the difference concepts between the Hebrew and Greek word for Glory.

"So the Hebrew concept of Glory is heavy or weighty. Like as a person can feel the weighty of honor, dignity or authority of a dignitary or a famous person or some one of authority that walks in the room. In this concept one can discern the change in the atmosphere of a place by another person.

In the Greek concept of Glory it is the reputation of the person or the splendor; or the brightness of a deity, person, or thing. Their personality releases a brightness or an aura of light, they actually lighten place or an atmosphere. With God it describes his exalted state or condition, pre-eminence. The best we can do is to describe the Glory of God as encompassing ALL of His Attributes. God's Glory is His Supreme, Incomparable Excellence." (Lauro Adame)

Another word is SHEKINAH which was the visible majesty of the Divine Presence, especially when resting or dwelling between the cherubim on the mercy seat, in the Tabernacle (Exodus 25:22).

The Hebrew word for BEAUTY (Psalm 27:4) is NOAM meaning splendor or grace. In Psalm 27:4 it is the worshipper that is allowed to gaze into the Beauty- Glory of God through their passionate unwavering love for His presence. The Beauty is translated Glory in Isaiah 61:3 from the Septuagint (the Greek Translation of the Old Testament) it says... *"To give those who mourn in Zion (Beauty) GLORY instead of ashes, oil of gladness to those who mourn; the garment of (Praise)*

GLORY instead of a spirit of indifference and depression."

The Hebrew word GA'OWN is the word for MAJESTY meaning: high, excellency, pride, pomp, swelling. This word describes the excellency of a king or dignitary, but connected God's Glory it describes how His Majesty swells high with the power of His excellency that it releases the Fear of the Lord upon all. So powerful is the Majesty of His Glory that man will either abhor and cast down their idols or hide themselves from the sheer fear of it. (Isaiah 2:10, 19, 21)

The Hebrew word 'ESH is the word for FIRE, referring to the Glory Fire of God. It means burning, fiery, flaming, hot, fire. When ever the GLORY FIRE of God shows up, it is for a few reasons, first it is for judgment (Numbers 11:1-3), secondly it is for protection (Exodus 13:21-22, Zechariah 2:5), thirdly for a sign of acceptance (2 Chronicles 7:1-3), fourthly for purification (Malachi 3:1- 3) and fifthly a sign of covenant and empowerment (Genesis 15:10-17, Acts 2:3) It is Jesus' desire for us to baptized with his Glory Fire. (Matthew 3:11-12, Luke 12:49) And God is consuming Fire. (Hebrews 12:29)

GLORICATION

As Protestants we are well acquitted with the doctrines of Justification and Sanctification, but there is a doctrine that we Western Christians need to be requited with and it is called the doctrine of Glorification. (John 17:10; Romans 8:17, 30; 2 Thessalonians 1:10,12)

This doctrine is strongly taught by our Eastern Orthodox brethren. This doctrine is a not a futurist doctrine but a present truth doctrine that teaches that all believers can be partakers in His Divine Nature, the Glory of God in this present life.

A brief synopsis of this doctrine is as the following. The Apostle Peter said…

" As His divine power (the Holy Spirit) has given to us all things that pertain to life and godliness, through the knowledge of Him(Christ Jesus) who called us by Glory and virtue, by which have been given to us exceedingly great and precious promises (the Word), that through these you may be partakers of the Divine Nature (the Glory of the Father)… "

2 Peter 1:3, 4

The Original purpose of Man was that he was made in the image and likeness of God to commune, carry, and release God's Glory. But because of sin that image and likeness was marred. God not only sent His only Begotten Son to save mankind from their sin but to restore the image and likeness of man back to God through the Image of His Son, the Lord Jesus Christ. The Son of God bringing back many sons into Glory (Hebrews 2:10)

It is by His incarnation, the Son of God who is the fullness of the Godhead inhabited human flesh, that we are joined to Christ, through faith, in holy baptism begin the process of a new creation, we become the sons of God and we allowed again the experience of deification, thereby being changed from glory to glory. (John 1:12, Colossians 2:9, 2 Corinthians 3:18, John 17:22-24)

This doctrine is best illustrated by the example of the fires of the blacksmith. The blacksmith takes a steel sword and puts it into the hot fires until the sword takes on a red glow. The energies of the fire interpenetrates the sword. The sword never becomes fire, but it picks up the same properties of fire. So because Christ is the fullness of God and God's Glory is Fire, when the believer is join to Christ, the humanity of the believer is interpenetrated with and by the energy fire of God's glory through Christ's glorified body. Thus we being human are destine to be glorified. (1 Corinthians 15:49; 3:18; 1 John 4:17; Romans 6:4)

The key verses for this Topical Bible are...

Habakkuk 2:14
"For the earth shall be filled with the knowledge of the **Glory** of the Lord, as the waters cover the sea,"

2 Corinthians 3:18
"But we all, with open face beholding as in a glass the **Glory of the Lord**, are changed into the same image from **glory to glory**, even as by the Spirit of the Lord,"

2 Chronicles 5:14
"So that the priests could not stand to minister by reason of the cloud: **for the Glory of the Lord had filled the house of God.**"

GLORY is RADIANCE, MAGNIFICENCE, BRILLIANCE, MAJESTY, SPLENDOR, and BEAUTY.

The Glory produces wealth, riches, honor, and prosperity. Glory brings salvation, healing, and restoration. Glory attracts. Glory promotes. Glory transforms. Glory releases miracles. Glory brings prosperity.

Angels live in the glory realm (Rev.18:1). Seraphim and cherubim live in the glory realm. Thunder and lightning are also manifestations of God's glory and strength.

Remember that we are all called to His GLORY.

"That ye would walk worthy of God, who hath called you unto his kingdom and **Glory**."
1 Thessalonians 2:12

"But the God of all grace, who hath called us unto **His Eternal Glory** by Christ Jesus, after that ye have suffered a while, make you perfect, stablish, strengthen, settle you."
1 Peter 5:10

"According as his divine power hath given unto us all things that pertain unto life and godliness, through the knowledge of him that **hath called us to glory and virtue:**"
2 Peter 1:3

THE GLORY IN THE OLD TESTAMENT

The Book of Genesis

Genesis 3 :8
And they heard the **voice of the Lord God walking** in the garden in the cool of the day: and Adam and his wife hid themselves from the **presence** of the Lord God amongst the trees of the garden.

Genesis 5:22
And **Enoch walked with God** after he begat Methuselah three hundred years, and begat sons and daughters:

Genesis 5:24
And Enoch walked with God : and he was not; for God took him.

Genesis 6:9
Noah was a just man and perfect in his generations, and **Noah walked with God .**

Genesis 12:7
And the LORD appeared unto Abram, and said, Unto thy seed will I give this land: and there builded he an altar unto the LORD, who appeared unto him.

Genesis 15:17-18
And it came to pass, that, when the sun went down, and it was dark, **behold a smoking furnace, and a burning lamp (The Glory-fire)**that passed between those pieces. In the same day the LORD made a covenant with Abram...

Genesis 17:1-2
And when Abram was ninety years old and nine, **the LORD appeared to Abram**, and said unto him, I am the Almighty God; walk before me, and be thou perfect. And I will make my covenant between me and thee, and will multiply thee exceedingly.

Genesis 18:1-2
And the LORD appeared unto him in the plains of Mamre: and he sat in the tent door in

the heat of the day; And he lift up his eyes and looked, and, lo, three men stood by him: and when he saw them, he ran to meet them from the tent door, and bowed himself toward the ground...

Genesis 26:2

And the LORD appeared unto him, and said, Go not down into Egypt; dwell in the land which I shall tell thee of:

Genesis 26:24-25

And the LORD appeared unto him the same night, and said, I am the God of Abraham thy father: fear not, for I am with thee, and will bless thee, and multiply thy seed for my servant Abraham's sake. And he builded an altar there, and called upon the name of the LORD and pitched his tent there:

The Book of Exodus

Exodus 3:2

And the angel of the LORD appeared unto him in a flame of fire out of the midst of a bush: and he looked, and, behold, the bush burned with fire, and the bush was not consumed.

Exodus 15 :6
Thy right hand, **O Lord, is become glorious in power: thy right hand**, O Lord, hath dashed in pieces the enemy.

Exodus 15 :11
Who is like unto thee, O Lord, among the gods? who is like thee, **glorious in holiness, fearful in praises**, doing wonders?

Exodus 15 :11 (Amplified)
"Who is like You among the gods, O Lord? Who is like You, **majestic in holiness, Awesome in splendor**, working wonders?

Exodus 15 :21
And Miriam answered them, Sing ye to the Lord, for he hath triumphed **gloriously**; the horse and his rider hath he thrown into the sea.

Exodus 16 :7
And in the morning, then **ye shall see the glory of the Lord;** for that he heareth your murmurings against the Lord: and what are we, that ye murmur against us?

Exodus 16 :10
And it came to pass, as Aaron spake unto the whole congregation of the children of Israel, that

they looked toward the wilderness, and, **behold, the glory of the Lord appeared in the cloud.**

Exodus 19 :16

And it came to pass on the third day in the morning, **that there were thunders and lightnings, and a thick cloud upon the mount**, and the voice of the trumpet exceeding loud; so that all the people that was in the camp trembled.

Exodus 20:18

And all the people saw **the thunderings, and the lightnings, and the noise of the trumpet, and the mountain smoking:** and when the people saw it, they removed, and stood afar off.

Exodus 24 :16

And the glory of the Lord abode upon mount Sinai, and the cloud covered it six days: and the seventh day he called unto Moses out of the midst of the cloud.

Exodus 24 :17 (Amplified)

In the sight of the Israelites **the appearance of the glory *and* brilliance of the Lord** was like **consuming fire on the top of the mountain.**

Exodus 24 :17
And the sight of **the glory of the Lord was like devouring fire on the top of the mount** in the eyes of the children of Israel.

Exodus 25 :22
And there **I will meet with thee, and I will commune with thee from above the mercy seat**, from between the two cherubims which are upon the ark of the testimony, of all things which I will give thee in commandment unto the children of Israel.

Exodus 28 :2
And thou shalt make holy garments for Aaron thy brother for **glory** and for beauty.

Exodus 28 :40
And for Aaron's sons thou shalt make coats, and thou shalt make for them girdles, and bonnets shalt thou make for them, **for glory and for beauty.**

Exodus 29 :43
And there I will meet with the children of Israel, and **the tabernacle shall be sanctified by my glory.**

Exodus 33:14-15
And he said, My **presence** shall go with thee, and I will give thee rest. And he said unto him, If thy **presence** go not with me, carry us not up hence.

Exodus 33 :14 (PAV)
Every where you go the Glory of My Presence will be with you always. And My Glory will give you rest, peace and prosperity.

Exodus 33 :18
And he said, I beseech thee, **shew me thy glory**.

Exodus 33 :22
And it shall come to pass, while **my glory passeth by, that I will put thee in a clift of the rock, and will cover thee with my hand while I pass by:**

Exodus 34:29-30
And it came to pass, when **Moses** came down from mount Sinai with the two tables of testimony in **Moses'** hand, when he came down from the mount, that **Moses** wist not that the **skin of his face shone while he talked with him.** And when Aaron and all the children of Israel saw **Moses, behold, the skin of his face**

shone; and they were afraid to come nigh him.

Exodus 34 :33
And till **Moses** had done speaking with them, he **put a vail on his face.**

Exodus 34 :35
And the children of Israel saw the **face** of **Moses, that the skin of Moses' face shone: and Moses put the vail upon his face again,** until he went in to speak with him.

Exodus 40:34
Then a cloud covered the tent of the congregation, **and the glory of the Lord filled the tabernacle.**

Exodus 40:34 (Amplified)
[*The Glory of the Lord*] **Then the cloud [the Shekinah, God's visible, dwelling presence]** covered the Tent of Meeting, and **the glory *and* brilliance of the Lord** filled the tabernacle.

Exodus 40:35
And Moses was not able to enter into the tent of the congregation, because the cloud abode thereon, **and the glory of the Lord filled the tabernacle.**

The Book of Leviticus

Leviticus 9:6
And Moses said, This is the thing which the Lord commanded that ye should do: **and the glory of the Lord shall appear unto you.**

Leviticus 9:23
And Moses and Aaron went into the tabernacle of the congregation, and came out, and blessed the people: **and the glory of the Lord appeared unto all the people.**

The Book of Numbers

Numbers 14:10
But all the congregation bade stone them with stones. **And the glory of the Lord** appeared in the tabernacle of the congregation before all the children of Israel.

Numbers 14:21
But as truly as I live, all the earth shall be filled with the glory of the Lord.

Numbers 14:22
Because all those men which have seen **my glory,** and my miracles, which I did in Egypt and in the wilderness, and have tempted me now

these ten times, and have not hearkened to my voice;

Numbers 16:19
And Korah gathered all the congregation against them unto the door of the tabernacle of the congregation: **and the glory of the Lord appeared unto all the congregation.**

Numbers 16:42
And it came to pass, when the congregation was gathered against Moses and against Aaron, that they looked toward the tabernacle of the congregation: and, behold, the cloud covered it, **and the glory of the Lord appeared.**

Numbers 20:6
And Moses and Aaron went from the presence of the assembly unto the door of the tabernacle of the congregation, and they fell upon their faces: **and the glory of the Lord appeared unto them.**

The Book of Deuteronomy

Deuteronomy 5:24
And ye said, Behold, the Lord our God hath shewed us **his glory** and his greatness, and we

have heard his voice out of the midst of the fire: we have seen this day that God doth talk with man, and he liveth.

Deuteronomy 28:58
If thou wilt not observe to do all the words of this law that are written in this book, that thou mayest fear this **glorious** and fearful name, The Lord Thy God;

Deuteronomy 31:15
And the LORD appeared in the tabernacle in a pillar of a cloud: and the pillar of the cloud stood over the door of the tabernacle.

Deuteronomy 33:2
And he said, **The Lord came from Sinai,** and rose up from Seir unto them; **he shined forth from mount Paran,** and he came with ten thousands of saints: from his right hand went a fiery law for them.

Deuteronomy 33:17
His glory is like the firstling of his bullock, and his horns are like the horns of unicorns: with them he shall push the people together to the ends of the earth: and they are the ten thousands of Ephraim, and they are the thousands of Manasseh.

The Books of 1 & 2 Samuel

1 Samuel 2:8
He raiseth up the poor out of the dust, and lifteth up the beggar from the dunghill, to set them among princes, and to make them inherit **the throne of glory**: for the pillars of the earth are the Lord's, and he hath set the world upon them.

1 Samuel 3:21
And the LORD appeared again in Shiloh: for **the LORD revealed himself to Samuel in Shiloh by the word of the LORD.**

1 Samuel 4:21
And she named the child Ichabod, saying, **The glory** is departed from Israel: because the ark of God was taken, and because of her father in law and her husband.

1 Samuel 4 :22
And she said, **The glory** is departed from Israel: for the ark of God is taken.

2 Samuel 22:13
Through the **brightness** before him were **coals of fire kindled.**

The Lord **thunder**ed from heaven, and the most High uttered his voice.

The Book of 1 Kings

1 Kings 3:5
In Gibeon **the LORD appeared** to Solomon in a dream by night: and God said, Ask what I shall give thee.

1 Kings 8:11
So that the priests could not stand to minister because of the cloud: **for the glory of the Lord had filled the house of the Lord.**

1 Kings 9:2
That **the LORD appeared** to Solomon the second time, as he had appeared unto him at Gibeon.

1 Kings 10:14 (Amplified)
[*Wealth,* **Splendor** *and Wisdom*] Now the weight of the gold that came to Solomon in one [particular] year was six hundred and sixty-six talents of gold...

1 Kings 18:38-39

Then **the fire of the LORD** fell, and consumed the burnt sacrifice, and the wood, and the stones, and the dust, and licked up the water that was in the trench. And when all the people saw it, they fell on their faces: and they said, The LORD, he is the God; the LORD, he is the God.

The Books of 1 & 2 Chronicles

1 Chronicles 16:10

Glory ye in his holy name: let the heart of them rejoice that seek the Lord.

1 Chronicles 16:24

Declare his glory among the heathen; his marvellous works among all nations.

1 Chronicles 16:27

Glory and honour are in his presence; strength and gladness are in his place.

1 Chronicles 16:28

Give unto the Lord, ye kindreds of the people, give unto the **Lord glory** and strength.

1 Chronicles 16:29
Give unto **the Lord the glory** due unto his name: bring an offering, and come before him: worship the Lord in the beauty of holiness.

1 Chronicles 16:29(Amplified)
Ascribe to the Lord the **glory** *and* **honor** due His name; Bring an offering [of thanksgiving], and come before Him; Worship the **Lord in the splendor of holiness.**

1 Chronicles 16:35
And say ye, Save us, O God of our salvation, and gather us together, and deliver us from the heathen, that we may give thanks to thy holy name, and **glory** in thy praise.

1 Chronicles 29:13
Now therefore, our God, we thank thee, and praise thy **glorious name.**

1 Chronicles 22:5
And David said, Solomon my son is young and tender, and the house that is to be builded for the Lord must be exceeding magnifical, **of fame and of glory throughout all countries:** I will therefore now make preparation for it. So David prepared abundantly before his death.

1 Chronicles 22:5 (Amplified)

David said, "Solomon my son is young and inexperienced, and the house that is to be built for the Lord shall be exceedingly magnificent, famous, and **an object of glory *and* splendor** throughout all lands [of the earth]. So now I will make preparations for it." Therefore, David made ample preparations before his death.

1 Chronicles 29:11

Thine, O Lord is the greatness, and the power, and the **glory**, and the victory, and the majesty: for all that is in the heaven and in the earth is thine; thine is the kingdom, O Lord, and thou art exalted as head above all.

1 Chronicles 29:25

And the Lord magnified Solomon exceedingly in the sight of all Israel, and bestowed upon him such **royal majesty** as had not been on any king before him in Israel.

2 Chronicles 5 :14

So that the priests could not stand to minister by reason of the cloud: **for the glory of the Lord** had filled the house of God.

2 Chronicles 7 :1
Now when Solomon had made an end of praying, the fire came down from heaven, and consumed the burnt offering and the sacrifices; and **the glory of the Lord** filled the house.

2 Chronicles 7:2
And the priests could not enter into the house of the Lord, because **the glory of the Lord had filled the Lord's house.**

2 Chronicles 7 :3
And when all the children of Israel saw how the fire came down, and **the glory of the Lord upon** the house, they bowed themselves with their faces to the ground upon the pavement, and worshipped, and praised the Lord, saying, For he is good; for his mercy endureth for ever.

2 Chronicles 7:12
And the LORD appeared to Solomon by night, and said unto him, I have heard thy prayer, and have chosen this place to myself for an house of sacrifice.

The Book of Nehemiah

Nehemiah 9:5
Then the Levites, Jeshua, and Kadmiel, Bani, Hashabniah, Sherebiah, Hodijah, Shebaniah, and

Pethahiah, said, Stand up and bless the Lord your God for ever and ever: and **blessed be thy glorious name,** which is exalted above all blessing and praise.

The Book of Esther

Esther 1:4
When he shewed the riches of **his glorious kingdom** and the honour of his excellent **majesty** many days, even an hundred and fourscore days.

The Book of Job

Job 19:9
He hath stripped me of my **glory**, and taken the crown from my head.

Job 29 :20
My **glory** was fresh in me, and my bow was renewed in my hand.

Job 37 :5
God **thundereth** marvellously with **his voice;** great things doeth he, which we cannot comprehend.

Job 40:9-10

Hast thou an arm like God? or canst thou **thunder with a voice** like him? Deck thyself now with majesty and excellency; and array thyself with glory and beauty.

The Book of Psalms

Psalm 3:3

But thou, O Lord, art a shield for me; **my glory**, and the lifter up of mine head.

Psalm 4:2

O ye sons of men, how long will ye turn **my glory** into shame? how long will ye love vanity, and seek after leasing? Selah.

Psalm 8:1

O Lord, our Lord, how excellent is thy name in all the earth! who hast set **thy glory** above the heavens.

Psalm 8:5

For thou hast made him a little lower than the angels, and hast **crowned him with glory** and honour.

Psalm 9:3

When mine enemies are turned back, they shall fall and perish at thy (**Glory**)**presence**.

Psalm 16:9

Therefore my heart is glad, and **my glory** rejoiceth: my flesh also shall rest in hope.

Psalm 16:11

Thou wilt shew me the path of life: in thy **presence** (**Glory**) is fullness of joy; at thy right hand there are pleasures for evermore.

Psalm 18:12

At the **brightness** that was before **him his thick clouds passed, hail stones and coals of fire**.

Psalm 19:1-3

The heavens declare **the glory of God**; and the firmament sheweth his handywork. Day unto day uttereth speech, and night unto night sheweth knowledge. There is no speech nor language, where their voice is not heard.

Psalm 21:5

His glory is great in thy salvation: **honour and majesty** hast thou laid upon him.

Psalm 24:7

Lift up your heads, O ye gates; and be ye lift up, ye everlasting doors; and **the King of glory** shall come in.

Psalm 24:8

Who is this **King of glory?** The Lord strong and mighty, the Lord mighty in battle.

Psalm 24:9

Lift up your heads, O ye gates; even lift them up, ye everlasting doors; and **the King of glory** shall come in.

Psalm 24:10

Who is this **King of glory?** **The Lord of hosts, he is the King of glory.** Selah.

Psalm 27:4

One thing have I desired of the Lord, that will I seek after; that I may dwell in the house of the Lord all the days of my life, to behold **the beauty (Glory) of the Lord**, and to enquire in his temple.

Psalm 27:4 (Amplified)

One thing I have asked of the Lord, and that I will seek: That I may dwell in the house of the Lord [in His presence] all the days of my life, To gaze upon the **beauty [the delightful loveliness and majestic grandeur] of the Lord** And to meditate in His temple.

Psalm 29:1
Give unto the Lord, O ye mighty, give unto the Lord **glory** and strength.

Psalm 29:2
Give unto the Lord the **glory** due unto his name; worship the Lord in the **beauty of holiness.**

Psalm 29:3
The voice of the Lord is upon the waters: **the God of glory thundereth**: the Lord is upon many waters.

Psalm 29:4
The voice of the Lord is powerful; the voice of the Lord is **full of majesty (Glory)**.

Psalm 29:9
The voice of the Lord maketh the hinds to calve, and discovereth the forests: and in his temple doth every one speak of **His Glory**.

Psalm 30:12
To the end that my **glory** may sing praise to thee, and not be silent. O Lord my God, I will give thanks unto thee for ever.

Psalm 31:20
Thou shalt hide them in the **secret of thy presence (Glory)** from the pride of man: thou shalt keep them secretly in a pavilion from the strife of tongues.

Psalm 34:5 (Amplified)
They looked to Him and were **radiant (with His glorious light)**; Their faces will never blush in shame *or* confusion.

Psalm 45:3-4
Gird thy sword upon thy thigh, O most mighty, with **thy glory and thy majesty**. And in **thy majesty** ride prosperously because of truth and meekness and righteousness; and thy right hand shall teach thee terrible things.

Psalm 45:13
The king's daughter is all **glorious** within: her clothing is of wrought gold.

Psalm 49:16
Be not thou afraid when one is made rich, when the **glory** of his house is increased;

Psalm 49:17
For when he dieth he shall carry nothing away: his **glory** shall not descend after him.

Psalm 50:2
Out of Zion, the **perfection of beauty**, God hath **shined (with His Glory)**.

Psalm 57:5
Be thou exalted, O God, above the heavens; let **thy glory** be above all the earth.

Psalm 57:8
Awake up, **my glory**; awake, psaltery and harp: I myself will awake early.

Psalm 57:11
Be thou exalted, O God, above the heavens: let **thy glory** be above all the earth.

Psalm 62:7
In God is my salvation and **my glory**: the rock of my strength, and my refuge, is in God.

Psalm 63:2
To see thy power and **thy glory**, so as I have seen thee in the sanctuary.

Psalm 63:11
But the king shall rejoice in God; every one that sweareth by him shall **glory**: but the mouth of them that speak lies shall be stopped.

Psalm 64:10
The righteous shall be glad in the Lord, and shall trust in him; and all the upright in heart shall **glory**.

Psalm 66:2
Sing forth the honour of his name: make his praise **glorious**.

Psalm 66:2 (Amplified)
Sing of **the honor *and* glory *and* magnificence** of His name; Make His praise glorious.

Psalm 67:1
God be merciful unto us, and bless us; and cause **his face to shine (His glorious face)** upon us; Selah.

Psalm 68:8

The earth shook, the heavens also dropped at the **presence (Glory)** of God: even Sinai itself was moved at the **presence** of God, the God of Israel.

Psalm 68:17

The chariots (glorious chariots) of God are twenty thousand, even thousands of **angels**: the Lord is among them, as in Sinai, in the holy place.

Psalm 72:19

And blessed be his glorious name for ever: and let the whole earth be filled with **his glory**; Amen, and Amen.

Psalm 73:24

Thou shalt guide me with thy counsel, and afterward receive me to **glory**.

Psalm 76:4

Thou art more **glorious** and excellent than the mountains of prey.

Psalm 77:18

The voice of thy thunder was in the heaven: **the lightnings lightened the world**: the earth trembled and shook.

Psalm 78:61
And delivered his strength into captivity, and his **glory** into the enemy's hand.

Psalm 79:9
Help us, O God of our salvation, for the **glory of thy name**: and deliver us, and purge away our sins, for thy name's sake.

Psalm 80:1
Give ear, O Shepherd of Israel, thou that leadest Joseph like a flock; thou that dwellest between the cherubims, **shine forth (with your Glory).**

Psalm 81:7
Thou calledst in trouble, and I delivered thee; I answered thee **in the secret place of thunder**: I proved thee at the waters of Meribah. Selah.

Psalm 84:11
For the Lord God is a sun and shield: the Lord will give grace and **glory**: no good thing will he withhold from them that walk uprightly.

Psalm 85:9
Surely his salvation is nigh them that fear him; that **glory** may dwell in our land.

Psalm 87:3

Glorious things are spoken of thee, O city of God. Selah.

Psalm 89:17

For thou art the **glory** of their strength: and in thy favour our horn shall be exalted.

Psalm 89 :44

Thou hast made **his glory** to cease, and cast his throne down to the ground.

Psalm 90:16

Let thy work appear unto thy servants, and **thy glory** unto their children.

Psalm 93:1

The Lord reigneth, he is clothed with **majesty (Glory)**; the Lord is clothed with strength, wherewith he hath girded himself: the world also is stablished, that it cannot be moved.

Psalm 93:1 (Amplified)

[*The Majesty of the Lord.*] The Lord reigns, He is clothed with **majesty *and* splendor**; The Lord has clothed and encircled Himself with strength; the world is firmly established, it cannot be moved.

Psalm 96:3
Declare **his glory** among the heathen, his wonders among all people.

Psalm 96:6-7
Honour and **majesty** are before him: strength and beauty are in his sanctuary. Give unto the Lord, O ye kindreds of the people, give unto the Lord **glory** and strength.

Psalm 96:8
Give unto the Lord the **glory** due unto his name: bring an offering, and come into his courts.

Psalm 96:9 (Amplified)
Worship the Lord in the **splendor (Glory)** of His holiness; Tremble [in submissive wonder] before Him, all the earth.

Psalm 97:5-6
The hills melted like wax at the **presence (Glory)** of the Lord, at the **presence (Glory)**of the Lord of the whole earth. The heavens declare his righteousness, and all the people **see his glory**.

Psalm 99:1
The Lord reigneth; let the people tremble: he sitteth between the **cherubim**s; let the earth be moved.

Psalm 102:15
So the heathen shall fear the name of the Lord, and all the kings of the earth **thy glory**.

Psalm 102:16
When the Lord shall build up Zion, he shall appear in **his glory**.

Psalm 104:1
Bless the Lord, O my soul. O Lord my God, thou art very great; thou art clothed with **honour** and **majesty**.

Psalm 104:1 (Amplified)
[*The Lord's Care over All His Works.*] Bless *and* affectionately praise the Lord, O my soul! O Lord my God, You are very great; You are clothed with **splendor** and **majesty**...

Psalm 104:31
The **glory of the Lord** shall endure for ever: the Lord shall rejoice in his works.

Psalm 105:3

Glory ye in his holy name: let the heart of them rejoice that seek the Lord.

Psalm 110:3 (Amplified)

Your people will offer themselves willingly [to participate in Your battle] in the day of Your power; In the **splendor (Glory)** of holiness, from the womb of the dawn, Your young men are to You as the dew.

Psalm 111:3

His work is honourable and **glorious**: and his righteousness endureth for ever.

Psalm 114:7

Tremble, thou earth, at the **presence (Glory)** of the Lord, at the **presence** of the God of Jacob;

Psalm 144:6

Cast forth **lightning**, and scatter them: shoot out thine arrows, and destroy them.

Psalm 145 :5

I will speak of **the glorious honour of thy majesty**, and of thy wondrous works.

Psalm 145:12
To make known to the sons of men his mighty acts, and **the glorious majesty of his kingdom.**

Psalm 104:2
Who coverest thyself with **light(Glory-light)** as with a garment: who stretchest out the heavens like a curtain:

Psalm 106:5
That I may see the good of thy chosen, that I may rejoice in the gladness of thy nation, that I may **glory** with thine inheritance.

Psalm 106:20
Thus they changed their **glory** into the similitude of an ox that eateth grass.

Psalm 108:1
O God, my heart is fixed; I will sing and give praise, even with **my glory.**

Psalm 108:5
Be thou exalted, O God, above the heavens: and **thy glory** above all the earth;

Psalm 113:4
The Lord is high above all nations, and **his glory** above the heavens.

Psalm 115 :1

Not unto us, O Lord, not unto us, but unto thy name give **glory**, for thy mercy, and for thy truth's sake.

Psalm 138:5

Yea, they shall sing in the ways of the Lord: for great is the **glory of the Lord.**

Psalm 145:11

They shall speak of the **glory of thy kingdom,** and talk of thy power;

Psalm 148:13

Let them praise the name of the Lord: for his name alone is excellent; **his glory** is above the earth and heaven.

Psalm 149:5

Let the saints be joyful in **glory**: let them sing aloud upon their beds.

The Book of Proverbs

Proverbs 3:35

The wise shall inherit **glory**: but shame shall be the promotion of fools.

Proverbs 4:9
She shall give to thine head an ornament of grace: **a crown of glory** shall she deliver to thee.

Proverbs 16:31
The hoary head is **a crown of glory**, if it be found in the way of righteousness.

Proverbs 17:6
Children's children are the crown of old men; and the **glory** of children are their fathers.

Proverbs 19:11
The discretion of a man deferreth his anger; and it is his **glory** to pass over a transgression.

Proverbs 20:29
The **glory** of young men is their strength: and the beauty of old men is the grey head.

Proverbs 25:2
It is the **glory** of God to conceal a thing: but the honour of kings is to search out a matter.

Proverbs 25:27
It is not good to eat much honey: so for men to search their own **glory** is not **glory**.

Proverbs 28:12

When righteous men do rejoice, there is great **glory**: but when the wicked rise, a man is hidden.

The Book of Isaiah

Isaiah 2:10

Enter into the rock, and hide thee in the dust, for fear of the Lord, and for the **glory of his majesty**.

Isaiah 2:19

And they shall go into the holes of the rocks, and into the caves of the earth, for fear of the Lord, and for **the glory of his majesty**, when he ariseth to shake terribly the earth.

Isaiah 2:21

To go into the clefts of the rocks, and into the tops of the ragged rocks, for fear of the Lord, and for **the glory of his majesty**, when he ariseth to shake terribly the earth.

Isaiah 4:2

In that day shall the branch of the Lord be beautiful and **glorious**, and the fruit of the earth shall be excellent and comely for them that are escaped of Israel.

Isaiah 4:5

And the Lord will create upon every dwelling place of mount Zion, and upon her assemblies, a cloud and smoke by day, and the shining of a flaming fire by night: for upon all the **glory** shall be a defence.

Isaiah 4:5 (Amplified)

then the Lord will create over the entire site of Mount Zion and over her assemblies, **a cloud by day, smoke, and the brightness of a flaming fire by night; for over all the glory *and* brilliance** will be a canopy [a defense, a covering of His divine love and protection].

Isaiah 5:14

Therefore hell hath enlarged herself, and opened her mouth without measure: and their **glory**, and their multitude, and their pomp, and he that rejoiceth, shall descend into it.

Isaiah 6:1-4

In the year that king Uzziah died I saw also the Lord sitting upon a throne, high and lifted up, and **his train (the fullness of His Glory and Power)** filled the temple. Above it stood the seraphims: each one had six wings; with twain he covered his face, and with twain he covered his feet, and with twain he did fly. And one cried unto another, and said, Holy, holy, holy, is the Lord of hosts: the whole earth is **full of his glory.** And the posts of the door moved at the voice of him that cried, and the house was **filled with smoke (of His Glory).**

Isaiah 6:6-7
Then flew one of the seraphims unto me, having a live coal in his hand, which he had taken with the tongs from off the altar: And he laid it upon my mouth, and said, Lo, this hath touched thy lips; and thine iniquity is taken away, and thy sin purged.

Isaiah 10:16
Therefore shall the Lord, the Lord of hosts, send among his fat ones leanness; and under **his glory** he shall kindle a burning like the burning of a fire.

Isaiah 11:10
And in that day there shall be a root of Jesse, which shall stand for an ensign of the people; to it shall the Gentiles seek: and his rest shall be **glorious.**

Isaiah 22:23
And I will fasten him as a nail in a sure place; and he shall be for a **glorious** throne to his father's house.

Isaiah 24:14
They shall lift up their voice, they shall sing for the **majesty of the Lord**, they shall cry aloud from the sea.

Isaiah 28:5
In that day shall the Lord of hosts be for **a crown of glory,** and for a diadem of beauty, unto the residue of his people,

Isaiah 30:30
And the Lord shall cause **his glorious voice** to be heard, and shall shew the lighting down of his arm, with the indignation of his anger, and with the flame of a devouring fire, with scattering, and tempest, and hailstones.

Isaiah 33:21
But there the **glorious** Lord will be unto us a place of broad rivers and streams; wherein shall go no galley with oars, neither shall gallant ship pass thereby.

Isaiah 35:2
It shall blossom abundantly, and rejoice even with joy and singing: the **glory** of Lebanon shall be given unto it, the excellency of Carmel and Sharon, they shall see the glory of the Lord, and the excellency of our God.

Isaiah 40:5
And the **glory of the Lord** shall be revealed, and all flesh shall see it together: for the mouth of the Lord hath spoken it.

Isaiah 41:16
Thou shalt fan them, and the wind shall carry them away, and the whirlwind shall scatter them: and thou shalt rejoice in the Lord, and shalt **glory** in the Holy One of Israel.

Isaiah 42:8
I am the Lord: that is my name: and **my glory** will I not give to another, neither my praise to graven images.

Isaiah 42:12
Let them give **glory** unto the Lord, and declare his praise in the islands.

Isaiah 43:7

Even every one that is called by my name: for I have created him for **my glory**, I have formed him; yea, I have made him.

Isaiah 45:25

In the Lord shall all the seed of Israel be justified, and shall **glory**.

Isaiah 46:13

I bring near my righteousness; it shall not be far off, and my salvation shall not tarry: and I will place salvation in Zion for Israel **my glory**.

Isaiah 49:5

And now, saith the Lord that formed me from the womb to be his servant, to bring Jacob again to him, Though Israel be not gathered, yet shall I be **glorious** in the eyes of the Lord, and my God shall be my strength.

Isaiah 55:5

Behold, thou shalt call a nation that thou knowest not, and nations that knew not thee shall run unto thee because of the Lord thy God, and for the Holy One of Israel; for he hath **glorified** thee.

Isaiah 58:8

Then shall thy light break forth as the morning, and thine health shall spring forth speedily: and thy righteousness shall go before thee; the **glory of the Lord** shall be thy reward.

Isaiah 59:19

So shall they fear the name of the Lord from the west, and **his glory** from the rising of the sun. When the enemy shall come in like a flood, the Spirit of the Lord shall lift up a standard against him.

Isaiah 60:1

Arise, shine; for thy light is come, and the **glory** of the Lord is risen upon thee.

Isaiah 60:2

For, behold, the darkness shall cover the earth, and gross darkness the people: but the Lord shall arise upon thee, and **his glory** shall be seen upon thee.

Isaiah 60:3

And the Gentiles shall come to thy light, and kings to the **brightness** of thy rising.

Isaiah 60:7
All the flocks of Kedar shall be gathered together unto thee, the rams of Nebaioth shall minister unto thee: they shall come up with acceptance on mine altar, **and I will glorify the house of my glory.**

Isaiah 60:9
Surely the isles shall wait for me, and the ships of Tarshish first, to bring thy sons from far, their silver and their gold with them, unto the name of the Lord thy God, and to the Holy One of Israel, because he hath **glorified** thee.

Isaiah 60:13
The **glory** of Lebanon shall come unto thee, the fir tree, the pine tree, and the box together, to beautify the place of my sanctuary; and **I will make the place of my feet glorious.**

Isaiah 60:19
The sun shall be no more thy light by day; neither for brightness shall the moon give light unto thee: but the Lord shall be unto thee an everlasting light, and **thy God thy glory**.

Isaiah 60:21
Thy people also shall be all righteous: they shall inherit the land for ever, the branch of my

planting, the work of my hands, that I may be **glorified**.

Isaiah 61:3 (Amplified)
To grant to those who mourn in Zion *the following*: To give them a turban instead of dust [on their heads, a sign of mourning], The oil of joy instead of mourning, The garment [expressive] of praise instead of a disheartened spirit. So they will be called the trees of righteousness [strong and **magnificent**, distinguished for integrity, justice, and right standing with God], **The planting of the Lord, that He may be glorified.**

Isaiah 61:3 (The Septuagint)
To give those who mourn in Zion **(Beauty) GLORY** instead of ashes, oil of gladness to those who mourn; **the garment of (Praise) GLORY** instead of a spirit of indifference and depression."

Isaiah 61 :6
But ye shall be named the Priests of the Lord: men shall call you the Ministers of our God: ye shall eat the riches of the Gentiles, and in their **glory** shall ye boast yourselves.

Isaiah 62:1
For Zion's sake will I not hold my peace, and for Jerusalem's sake I will not rest, until the righteousness thereof go forth as **brightness**, and the salvation thereof as a lamp that burneth.

Isaiah 62:2
And the Gentiles shall see thy righteousness, and all kings **thy glory**: and thou shalt be called by a new name, which the mouth of the Lord shall name.

Isaiah 62:3
Thou shalt also be **a crown of glory** in the hand of the Lord, and a royal diadem in the hand of thy God.

Isaiah 63:1
Who is this that cometh from Edom, with dyed garments from Bozrah? this that is **glorious** in his apparel, travelling in the greatness of his strength? I that speak in righteousness, mighty to save.

Isaiah 63:12
That led them by the right hand of Moses with **his glorious arm**, dividing the water before them, to make himself an everlasting name?

Isaiah 63:14

As a beast goeth down into the valley, the Spirit of the Lord caused him to rest: so didst thou lead thy people, to make thyself a **glorious name**.

Isaiah 63:15

Look down from heaven, and behold from the habitation of thy holiness and of **thy glory**: where is thy zeal and thy strength, the sounding of thy bowels and of thy mercies toward me? are they restrained?

Isaiah 64:1-4

Oh that thou wouldest rend the heavens, that thou wouldest come down, that the mountains might flow down at thy **presence**, As when the melting fire burneth, the fire causeth the waters to boil, to make thy name known to thine adversaries, that the nations may tremble at thy **presence**! When thou didst terrible things which we looked not for, thou camest down, the mountains flowed down at thy **presence**.

Isaiah 66:12

For thus saith the Lord, Behold, I will extend peace to her like a river, and the **glory** of the Gentiles like a flowing stream: then shall ye suck, ye shall be borne upon her sides, and be dandled upon her knees.

Isaiah 66:18

For I know their works and their thoughts: it shall come, that I will gather all nations and tongues; and they shall come, and see **my glory**.

Isaiah 66:19

And I will set a sign among them, and I will send those that escape of them unto the nations, to Tarshish, Pul, and Lud, that draw the bow, to Tubal, and Javan, to the isles afar off, that have not heard my fame, neither have seen **my glory**; and they shall declare **my glory** among the Gentiles.

The Book of Jeremiah

Jeremiah 9:23-24

Thus saith the Lord, Let not the wise man **glory** in his wisdom, neither let the mighty man **glory** in his might, let not the rich man **glory** in his riches: But let him that glorieth **glory** in this, that he understandeth and knoweth me, that I am the Lord which exercise lovingkindness, judgment, and righteousness, in the earth: for in these things I delight, saith the Lord.

Jeremiah 13 :16

Give **glory** to the Lord your God, before he cause darkness, and before your feet stumble upon the dark mountains, and, while ye look for light, he turn it into the shadow of death, and make it gross darkness.

Jeremiah 13:18

Say unto the king and to the queen, Humble yourselves, sit down: for your principalities shall come down, even the crown of your **glory**.

Jeremiah 31 :12 (Amplified)

"They will come and sing aloud *and* shout for joy on the height of Zion, And will be **radiant** [with joy] over the goodness of the Lord— For the grain, for the new wine, for the oil, And for the young of the flock and the herd. And their life will be like a watered garden, And they shall never sorrow *or* languish again.

The Book of Ezekiel

Ezekiel 1:4

And I looked, and, behold, a whirlwind came out of the north, a great cloud, and a fire infolding itself, and a **brightness** was about it, and out of the midst thereof as the color of amber, out of the midst of the fire.

Ezekiel 1:13-14
As for the likeness of the living creatures, their appearance was like burning coals of fire, and like the appearance of lamps: it went up and down among the living creatures; and the **fire was bright**, and out of the **fire went forth lightning**. And the living creatures ran and returned as the appearance of a flash of **lightning**.

Ezekiel 1:27
And I saw as the color of amber, as the **appearance of fire** round about within it, from the appearance of his loins even upward, and from the appearance of his loins even downward, I saw as it were the **appearance of fire**, and it had **brightness round about**.

Ezekiel 1:28
As the appearance of the bow that is in the cloud in the day of rain, so was the appearance of the brightness round about. This was the **appearance of the likeness of the glory of the Lord**. And when I saw it, I fell upon my face, and I heard a voice of one that spake.

Ezekiel 3:12

Then the spirit took me up, and I heard behind me a voice of a great rushing, saying, Blessed be the **glory of the Lord** from his place.

Ezekiel 3:23

Then I arose, and went forth into the plain: and, behold, the **glory of the Lord** stood there, as the **glory** which I saw by the river of Chebar: and I fell on my face.

Ezekiel 8:2

Then I beheld, and lo a likeness as the **appearance of fire**: from the appearance of his loins even downward, **fire**; and from his loins even upward, as the appearance of **brightness**, as the color of amber.

Ezekiel 8:4

And, behold, the **glory of the God** of Israel was there, according to the vision that I saw in the plain.

Ezekiel 9:3

And the **glory of the God** of Israel was gone up from the cherub, whereupon he was, to the threshold of the house. And he called to the man clothed with linen, which had the writer's inkhorn by his side;

Ezekiel 10:4
Then **the glory of the Lord** went up from the cherub, and stood over the threshold of the house; and the house was filled with the cloud, and the **court was full of the brightness of the Lord's glory.**

Ezekiel 10:18
Then **the glory of the Lord** departed from off the threshold of the house, and stood over the cherubims.

Ezekiel 10:19
And the cherubims lifted up their wings, and mounted up from the earth in my sight: when they went out, the wheels also were beside them, and every one stood at the door of the east gate of the Lord's house; and **the glory of the God** of Israel was over them above.

Ezekiel 11:22
Then did the cherubims lift up their wings, and the wheels beside them; and **the glory of the God** of Israel was over them above.

Ezekiel 11:23
And **the glory of the Lord** went up from the midst of the city, and stood upon the mountain which is on the east side of the city.

Ezekiel 39:21
And I will set **my glory** among the heathen, and all the heathen shall see my judgment that I have executed, and my hand that I have laid upon them.

Ezekiel 43:2
And, behold, **the glory of the God** of Israel came from the way of the east: and his voice was like a noise of many waters: and the **earth shined with his glory.**

Ezekiel 43:4
And **the glory of the Lord** came into the house by the way of the gate whose prospect is toward the east.

Ezekiel 43:5
So the spirit took me up, and brought me into the inner court; and, behold, **the glory of the Lord filled the house.**

Ezekiel 44:4
Then brought he me the way of the north gate before the house: and I looked, and, behold, **the glory of the Lord filled the house of the Lord: and I fell upon my face.**

The Book of Daniel

Daniel 4:36
At the same time my reason returned unto me; and for the glory of my kingdom, mine honour and brightness returned unto me; and my counselors and my lords sought unto me; and I was established in my kingdom, and **excellent majesty** was added unto me.

Daniel 5:19
And for the **majesty** that he gave him, all people, nations, and languages, trembled and feared before him: whom he would he slew; and whom he would he kept alive; and whom he would he set up; and whom he would he put down.

Daniel 7:14
And there was given him dominion, and **glory**, and a kingdom, that all people, nations, and languages, should serve him: his dominion is an everlasting dominion, which shall not pass away, and his kingdom that which shall not be destroyed.

Daniel 12:3
And they that be wise shall shine as the **brightness** of the firmament; and they that turn

many to righteousness as the stars for ever and ever.

The Book of Jonah

Jonah 1:3
But Jonah rose up to flee unto Tarshish from the **presence (Glory)**of the Lord, and went down to Joppa; and he found a ship going to Tarshish: so he paid the fare thereof, and went down into it, to go with them unto Tarshish from the **presence (Glory)**of the Lord.

Jonah 1:10
Then were the men exceedingly afraid, and said unto him. Why hast thou done this? For the men knew that he fled from the **presence (Glory)** of the Lord, because he had told them.

The Book of Nahum

Nahum 1:5
The mountains quake at him, and the hills melt, and the earth is burned at his **presence (Glory)**, yea, the world, and all that dwell therein.

The Book of Habakkuk

Habakkuk 2:14
For the earth shall be filled with **the knowledge of the glory of the Lord,** as the waters cover the sea.

Habakkuk 3:3 (Amplified)
God [approaching from Sinai] comes from Teman (Edom), And the Holy One from Mount Paran. Selah (pause, and calmly think of that). His **splendor (Glory)** *and* **majesty** covers the heavens And the earth is full of His praise.

Habakkuk 3:4
And his brightness was as the **light (Glory-light)**; he had horns coming out of his hand: and there was the hiding of his power.

The Book of Zephaniah

Zephaniah 1:7
Hold thy peace at the **presence(Glory) of the Lord God**: for the day of the Lord is at hand: for the Lord hath prepared a sacrifice, he hath bid his guests.

The Book of Haggai

Haggai 1:8
Go up to the mountain, and bring wood, and build the house; and I will take pleasure in it, and I will be **glorified**, saith the Lord.

Haggai 2:7
And I will shake all nations, and the desire of all nations shall come: and I will fill this house with **glory**, saith the Lord of hosts.

Haggai 2:9
The **glory** of this latter house shall be greater than of the former, saith the Lord of hosts: and in this place will I give peace, saith the Lord of hosts.

The Book of Zechariah

Zechariah 2:5
For I, saith the Lord, will be unto her **a wall of fire (Glory-fire)** round about, and will be the **glory** in the midst of her.
Zechariah 2:8
For thus saith the Lord of hosts; After the **glory** hath he sent me unto the nations which spoiled

you: for he that toucheth you toucheth the apple of his eye.

Zechariah 6:13
Even he shall build the temple of the Lord; and he shall bear the **glory**, and shall sit and rule upon his throne; and he shall be a priest upon his throne: and the counsel of peace shall be between them both.

Zechariah 9:14
And the Lord shall be seen over them, and his arrow shall go forth as the **lightning**: and the Lord God shall blow the trumpet, and shall go with whirlwinds of the south.

Zechariah 10:1
Ask ye of the Lord rain in the time of the latter rain; so the Lord shall make **bright clouds (Glory-cloud),** and give them showers of rain, to every one grass in the field.

Zechariah 12:7
The Lord also shall save the tents of Judah first, that the **glory** of the house of David and the **glory** of the inhabitants of Jerusalem do not magnify themselves against Judah.

The Book of Malachi

Malachi 2:2

If ye will not hear, and if ye will not lay it to heart, to give **glory** unto my name, saith the Lord of hosts, I will even send a curse upon you, and I will curse your blessings: yea, I have cursed them already, because ye do not lay it to heart.

Malachi 3:2

But who may abide the day of His coming? And who shall stand when he appeareth? For He is like a refiner's fire, and like fuller's soap.

Malachi 3:3

And He shall sit as a refiner and purifier of silver: and He shall purify the sons of Levi. And purge them as gold and silver, that they may offer unto the Lord an offering of righteousness.

John Eckhardt

THE GLORY IN
THE NEW TESTAMENT

Matthew 3:11
I indeed baptize you with water unto repentance: but he that cometh after me is mightier than I, whose shoes I am not worthy to bear: **he shall baptize you with the Holy Ghost, and with fire** :

Matthew 4:8
Again, the devil taketh him up into an exceeding high mountain, and sheweth him all the kingdoms of the world, and the **glory** of them;

Matthew 6:2
Therefore when thou doest thine alms, do not sound a trumpet before thee, as the hypocrites do in the synagogues and in the streets, that they

may have **glory** of men. Verily I say unto you, They have their reward.

Matthew 6:13

And lead us not into temptation, but deliver us from evil: For thine is the kingdom, and the power, and the **glory**, for ever. Amen.

Matthew 6:29

And yet I say unto you, That even Solomon in all his **glory** was not arrayed like one of these.

Matthew 16:27

For the Son of man shall come in the **glory of his Father** with his angels; and then he shall reward every man according to his works.

Matthew 17:5

While he yet spake, behold, **a bright cloud overshadowed them**: and behold a voice out of the cloud, which said, This is my beloved Son, in whom I am well pleased; hear ye him.

Matthew 19:28

And Jesus said unto them, Verily I say unto you, That ye which have followed me, in the regeneration when the **Son of man shall sit in the throne of his glory,** ye also shall sit upon twelve thrones, judging the twelve tribes of Israel.

Matthew 24:30
And then shall appear the sign of the Son of man in heaven: and then shall all the tribes of the earth mourn, and they shall see the **Son of man coming in the clouds of heaven with power and great glory.**

Matthew 25:31
When the **Son of man shall come in his glory,** and all the holy angels with him, then shall he sit upon the **throne of his glory:**

Matthew 28:2-4
And, behold, there was a great earthquake: for the angel of the Lord descended from heaven, and came and rolled back the stone from the door, and sat upon it. **His countenance was like lightning, and his raiment white as snow:** And for fear of him the keepers did shake, and became as dead men.

The Book of Mark

Mark 8:38
Whosoever therefore shall be ashamed of me and of my words in this adulterous and sinful generation; of him also shall the Son of man be ashamed, when he cometh in **the glory of his Father** with the holy angels.

Mark 9:3 (Amplified)
and His clothes became **radiant *and* dazzling,** intensely white, as no launderer on earth can whiten them.

Mark 10:37
They said unto him, Grant unto us that we may sit, one on thy right hand, and the other on thy left hand, in thy **glory**.

Mark 13:26
And then shall they see the Son of man coming in the clouds with great power and **glory**.

The Book of Luke

Luke 1:19
And the angel answering said unto him, I am Gabriel, that stand in **the presence of God**; and am sent to speak unto thee, and to shew thee these glad tidings.

Luke 2:9
And, lo, the angel of the Lord came upon them, and **the glory of the Lord** shone round about them: and they were sore afraid.

Luke 2:14
Glory to God in the highest, and on earth peace, good will toward men.

Luke 2:32
A light to lighten the Gentiles, and the **glory** of thy people Israel.

Luke 3:16-17
John answered, saying unto them all, I indeed baptize you with water; but one mightier than I cometh, the latchet of whose shoes I am not worthy to unloose: **he shall baptize you with the Holy Ghost and with fire :**

Whose fan is in his hand, and he will throughly purge his floor, and will gather the wheat into his garner; but the chaff he will burn with **fire unquenchable.**

Luke 4:6
And the devil said unto him, All this power will I give thee, and the **glory** of them: for that is delivered unto me; and to whomsoever I will I give it.

Luke 4:15
And he taught in their synagogues, being **glorified** of all.

Luke 5:26
And they were all amazed, and they **glorified** God, and were filled with fear, saying, We have seen strange things to day.

Luke 7:16
And there came a fear on all: and they **glorified** God, saying, That a great prophet is risen up among us; and, That God hath visited his people.

Luke 9:26
For whosoever shall be ashamed of me and of my words, of him shall the Son of man be

ashamed, when he shall come in his own **glory**, and in his Father's, and of the holy angels.

Luke 9:31
Who appeared in **glory**, and spake of his decease which he should accomplish at Jerusalem.

Luke 9:32
But Peter and they that were with him were heavy with sleep: and when they were awake, they saw **his glory**, and the two men that stood with him.

Luke 11:36
If thy whole body therefore be **full of light**, having no part dark, the whole shall be **full of light, as when the bright shining of a candle doth give thee light.**

Luke 12:27
Consider the lilies how they grow: they toil not, they spin not; and yet I say unto you, that Solomon in all his **glory** was not arrayed like one of these.

Luke 12:49
I am come to send **fire (Glory-Fire)** on the earth; and what will I if it be already kindled?

Luke 13:13
And he laid his hands on her: and immediately she was made straight, and **glorified** God.

Luke 13:17
And when he had said these things, all his adversaries were ashamed: and all the people rejoiced for all the **glorious** things that were done by him.

Luke 17:15
And one of them, when he saw that he was healed, turned back, and with a loud voice **glorified** God,

Luke 17:18
There are not found that returned to give **glory** to God, save this stranger.

Luke 19:38
Saying, Blessed be the King that cometh in the name of the Lord: peace in heaven, and **glory** in the highest.

Luke 21:27
And then shall they see the Son of man coming in a cloud with power and **great glory**.

Luke 23:47

Now when the centurion saw what was done, he **glorified** God, saying, Certainly this was a righteous man.

Luke 24:26

Ought not Christ to have suffered these things, and to enter into **his glory**?

The Book of John

John 1:14

And the Word was made flesh, and dwelt among us, (and we beheld his **glory**, the **glory** as of the only begotten of the Father,) full of grace and truth.

John 2:11

This beginning of miracles did Jesus in Cana of Galilee, and manifested forth his **glory**; and his disciples believed on him.

John 7:18

He that speaketh of himself seeketh his own **glory**: but he that seeketh his **glory** that sent him, the same is true, and no unrighteousness is in him.

John 8:50
And I seek not mine own **glory**: there is one that seeketh and judgeth.

John 11:4
When Jesus heard that, he said, This sickness is not unto death, but for the **glory of God**, that the Son of God might be glorified thereby.

John 11:40
Jesus saith unto her, Said I not unto thee, that, if thou wouldest believe, thou shouldest see the **glory of God?**

John 12:16
These things understood not his disciples at the first: but when Jesus was **glorified**, then remembered they that these things were written of him, and that they had done these things unto him.

John 12:23
And Jesus answered them, saying, The hour is come, that the Son of man should be **glorified**.

John 12:28
Father, glorify thy name. Then came there a voice from heaven, saying, I have both **glorified** it, and will glorify it again.

John 12:41
These things said Isaiah, when he saw **his glory**, and spake of him.

John 14:13
And whatsoever ye shall ask in my name, that will I do, that the Father may be **glorified** in the Son.

John 15:8
Herein is my Father **glorified**, that ye bear much fruit; so shall ye be my disciples.

John 17:4
I have **glorified** thee on the earth: I have finished the work which thou gavest me to do.

John 17:5
And now, O Father, glorify thou me with thine own self with the **glory** which I had with thee before the world was.

John 17:10
And all mine are thine, and thine are mine; and I am **glorified** in them.

John 17:22

And the **glory** which thou gavest me I have given them; that they may be one, even as we are one:

John17:24

Father, I will that they also, whom thou hast given me, be with me where I am; that they may behold **my glory**, which thou hast given me: for thou lovedst me before the foundation of the world.

The Book of Acts

Acts 2:2-4

And suddenly there came a sound from heaven as of a rushing mighty wind, and it filled all the house where they were sitting. And there appeared unto them **cloven tongues like as of fire,** and it sat upon each of them. And they were all filled with the Holy Ghost, and began to speak with other tongues, as the Spirit gave them utterance.

Acts 3:13

The God of Abraham, and of Isaac, and of Jacob, the God of our fathers, hath **glorified his Son Jesus**; whom ye delivered up, and denied him in the presence of Pilate, when he was determined to let him go.

Acts 7:2
And he said, Men, brethren, and fathers, hearken; **The God of glory** appeared unto our father Abraham, when he was in Mesopotamia, before he dwelt in Charran,

Acts 7:55
But he, being full of the Holy Ghost, looked up steadfastly into heaven, and saw **the glory of God, and Jesus standing on the right hand of God,**

Acts 12:23
And immediately the angel of the Lord smote him, because he gave not God the **glory**: and he was eaten of worms, and gave up the ghost.

Acts 22:11
And when I could not see for the **glory of that light**, being led by the hand of them that were with me, I came into Damascus.

Acts 26:13
At midday, O king, I saw in the way **a light from heaven, above the brightness of the sun,**

shining round about me and them which journeyed with me.

The Book of Romans

Romans 1:23
And changed the **glory** of the uncorruptible God into an image made like to corruptible man, and to birds, and fourfooted beasts, and creeping things.

Romans 2:7
To them who by patient continuance in well doing seek for **glory and honour and immortality, eternal life:**

Romans 2:10
But **glory**, honour, and peace, to every man that worketh good, to the Jew first, and also to the Gentile:

Romans 3:23
For all have sinned, and come short of the **glory of God;**

Romans 4:2
For if Abraham were justified by works, he hath whereof to **glory**; but not before God.

Romans 4:20
He staggered not at the promise of God through unbelief; but was strong in faith, giving **glory** to God;

Romans 5:2
By whom also we have access by faith into this grace wherein we stand, and rejoice in hope of **the glory of God.**

Romans 8:17
And if children, then heirs; heirs of God, and joint-heirs with Christ; if so be that we suffer with him, that we may be also **glorified** together.

Romans 8:18
For I reckon that the sufferings of this present time are not worthy to be compared with the **glory** which shall be revealed in us.

Romans 8:21
Because the creature itself also shall be delivered from the bondage of corruption into the **glorious** liberty of the children of God.

Romans 8:30
Moreover whom he did predestinate, them he also called: and whom he called, them he also

justified: and whom he justified, them he also **glorified**.

Romans 9:4
Who are Israelites; to whom pertaineth the adoption, and the **glory**, and the covenants, and the giving of the law, and the service of God, and the promises;

Romans 9:23
And that he might make known the riches **of his glory** on the vessels of mercy, which he had afore prepared unto **glory**,

Romans 11:36
For of him, and through him, and to him, are all things: to whom be **glory** for ever. Amen.

Romans 15:7
Wherefore receive ye one another, as Christ also received us to **the glory of God.**

Romans 16:27
To God only wise, be **glory** through Jesus Christ for ever. Amen.

The Books of 1 & 2 Corinthians

1 Corinthians 1:29
That no flesh should **glory** in his presence.

1 Corinthians 1:31
That, according as it is written, He that glorieth, let him **glory** in the Lord.

1 Corinthians 2:7
But we speak the wisdom of God in a mystery, even the hidden wisdom, which God ordained before the world unto our **glory**:

1 Corinthians 2:8
Which none of the princes of this world knew: for had they known it, they would not have crucified **the Lord of glory**.

1 Corinthians 3:21
Therefore let no man **glory** in men. For all things are your's;

1 Corinthians 4:7
For who maketh thee to differ from another? and what hast thou that thou didst not receive? now if thou didst receive it, why dost thou **glory**, as if thou hadst not received it?

1 Corinthians 5:6
Your **glorying** is not good. Know ye not that a little leaven leaveneth the whole lump?

1 Corinthians 9:16
For though I preach the gospel, I have nothing to **glory** of: for necessity is laid upon me; yea, woe is unto me, if I preach not the gospel!

1 Corinthians 10:31
Whether therefore ye eat, or drink, or whatsoever ye do, do all to the **glory of God**.

1 Corinthians 15:40
There are also celestial bodies, and bodies terrestrial: but the **glory** of the celestial is one, and the **glory** of the terrestrial is another.

1 Corinthians 15:41
There is one **glory** of the sun, and another **glory** of the moon, and another **glory** of the stars: for one star differeth from another star in **glory**.

1 Corinthians 15:43
It is sown in dishonour; it is raised in **glory**: it is sown in weakness; it is raised in power:

2 Corinthians 1:20
For all the promises of God in him are yea, and in him Amen, unto the **glory of God** by us.

2 Corinthians 3:7
But if the ministration of death, written and engraven in stones, was glorious, so that the children of Israel could not stedfastly behold the face of Moses for the **glory** of his countenance; which **glory** was to be done away:

2 Corinthians 3:8
How shall not the ministration of the spirit be rather **glorious**?

2 Corinthians 3:9
For if the ministration of condemnation be **glory**, much more doth the ministration of righteousness exceed in **glory**.

2 Corinthians 3:10
For even that which was made glorious had no **glory** in this respect, by reason of the **glory** that excelleth.

2 Corinthians 3:18
But we all, with open face beholding as in a glass the **glory** of the Lord, are changed into the same

image from **glory** to **glory**, even as by the Spirit of the Lord.

2 Corinthians 4:7 (Amplified)

But we have this *precious* treasure [the good news about salvation] in [unworthy] earthen vessels [of human frailty], so that the **grandeur** *and* surpassing greatness of the power will be [shown to be] from God [His sufficiency] and not from ourselves.

2 Corinthians 4:6

For God, who commanded the light to shine out of darkness, hath shined in our hearts, to give the light of the knowledge of **the glory of God in the face of Jesus Christ.**

2 Corinthians 4:15

For all things are for your sakes, that the abundant grace might through the thanksgiving of many redound to the **glory** of God.

2 Corinthians 4:17

For our light affliction, which is but for a moment, worketh for us a far more exceeding and eternal weight of **glory;**

2 Corinthians 10:17

But he that glorieth, let him **glory** in the Lord.

2 Corinthians 11:30
If I must needs **glory**, I will **glory** of the things which concern mine infirmities.

2 Corinthians 12:1
It is not expedient for me doubtless to **glory**. I will come to visions and revelations of the Lord.

2 Corinthians 12:5
Of such an one will I **glory**: yet of myself I will not **glory**, but in mine infirmities.

2 Corinthians 12:6
For though I would desire to **glory**, I shall not be a fool; for I will say the truth: but now I forbear, lest any man should think of me above that which he seeth me to be, or that he heareth of me.

2 Corinthians 12:9
And he said unto me, My grace is sufficient for thee: for my strength is made perfect in weakness. Most gladly therefore will I rather **glory** in my infirmities, that the power of Christ may rest upon me.

2 Corinthians 12:11
I am become a fool in glorying; ye have compelled me: for I ought to have been

commended of you: for in nothing am I behind the very chiefest apostles, though I be nothing.

The Book of Galatians

Galatians 1:5
To whom be **glory** for ever and ever. Amen.

Galatians 5:26
Let us not be desirous of vain **glory**, provoking one another, envying one another.

Galatians 6:13
For neither they themselves who are circumcised keep the law; but desire to have you circumcised, that they may **glory** in your flesh.

Galatians 6:14
But God forbid that I should **glory**, save in the cross of our Lord Jesus Christ, by whom the world is crucified unto me, and I unto the world.

The Book of Ephesians

Ephesians 1:6
To the praise of **the glory of his grace**, wherein he hath made us accepted in the beloved.

Ephesians 1:14
Which is the earnest of our inheritance until the redemption of the purchased possession, unto **the praise of his glory**.

Ephesians 1:17
That the God of our Lord Jesus Christ, **the Father of glory**, may give unto you the spirit of wisdom and revelation in the knowledge of him:

Ephesians 1:18
The eyes of your understanding being enlightened; that ye may know what is the hope of his calling, and what **the riches of the glory** of his inheritance in the saints,

Ephesians 3:16
That he would grant you, according to **the riches of his glory**, to be strengthened with might by his Spirit in the inner man;

Ephesians 3:21
Unto him be **glory** in the church by Christ Jesus throughout all ages, world without end. Amen.

Ephesians 5:27
That he might present it to himself a **glorious** church, not having spot, or wrinkle, or any such

thing; but that it should be holy and without blemish.

The Book of Philippians

Philippians 1:11
Being filled with the fruits of righteousness, which are by Jesus Christ, unto the **glory** and praise of God.

Philippians 2:11
And that every tongue should confess that Jesus Christ is Lord, to the **glory of God the Father.**

Philippians 3:21
Who shall change our vile body, that it may be fashioned like unto his **glorious body,** according to the working whereby he is able even to subdue all things unto himself.

Philippians 4:19
But my God shall supply all your need according to his riches in **glory** by Christ Jesus.

Philippians 4:20
Now unto God and our Father be **glory** for ever and ever. Amen.

The Book of Colossians

Colossians 1:11
Strengthened with all might, according to **his glorious power**, unto all patience and longsuffering with joyfulness;

Colossians 1:27
To whom God would make known what is the riches of the **glory** of this mystery among the Gentiles; which **is Christ in you, the hope of glory:**

Colossians 3:4
When Christ, who is our life, shall appear, then shall ye also appear with him in **glory**.

The Books of 1 & 2 Thessalonians

1 Thessalonians 2:6
Nor of men sought we **glory**, neither of you, nor yet of others, when we might have been burdensome, as the apostles of Christ.

1 Thessalonians 2:12
That ye would walk worthy of God, who hath **called you unto his kingdom and glory.**

1 Thessalonians 2:20
For ye are our **glory** and joy.

2 Thessalonians 1:4
So that we ourselves **glory** in you in the churches of God for your patience and faith in all your persecutions and tribulations that ye endure:

2 Thessalonians 1:9
Who shall be punished with everlasting destruction from the presence of the Lord, and from **the glory of his power;**

2 Thessalonians 1:10
When he shall come to be **glorified** in his saints, and to be admired in all them that believe (because our testimony among you was believed) in that day.

2 Thessalonians 1:12
That the name of our Lord Jesus Christ may be **glorified** in you, and ye in him, according to the grace of our God and the Lord Jesus Christ.

2 Thessalonians 2:8
And then shall that Wicked be revealed, whom the Lord shall consume with the spirit of his mouth, and shall destroy with the **brightness of his coming:**

2 Thessalonians 2:14
Whereunto he called you by our gospel, to the obtaining of the **glory of our Lord Jesus Christ**.

2 Thessalonians 3:1
Finally, brethren, pray for us, that the word of the Lord may have free course, and be **glorified**, even as it is with you:

The Books of 1 & 2 Timothy

1 Timothy 1:11
According to the **glorious** gospel of the blessed God, which was committed to my trust.

1 Timothy 1:17
Now unto the King eternal, immortal, invisible, the only wise God, be honour and **glory** for ever and ever. Amen.

1 Timothy 3:16
And without controversy great is the mystery of godliness: God was manifest in the flesh, justified in the Spirit, seen of angels, preached unto the Gentiles, believed on in the world, received up into **glory**.

1 Timothy 6:16
Who only hath immortality, dwelling in the **light (Glory-light)** which no man can approach unto; whom no man hath seen, nor can see: to whom be honour and power everlasting. Amen.

2 Timothy 2:10
Therefore I endure all things for the elect's sakes, that they may also obtain the salvation which is in Christ Jesus with **eternal glory**.

2 Timothy 4:18
And the Lord shall deliver me from every evil work, and will preserve me unto his heavenly kingdom: to whom be **glory** for ever and ever. Amen.

The Book of Hebrews

Hebrews 1:3
Who being the **brightness of his glory**, and the express image of his person, and upholding all things by the word of his power, when he had by himself purged our sins, sat down on the right hand of the **Majesty on high:**

Hebrews 1:7
And of the angels he saith, Who maketh his angels spirits, and his ministers **a flame of fire.**

Hebrews 2:7

Thou madest him a little lower than the angels; thou crownest him with **glory and honour**, and didst set him over the works of thy hands:

Hebrews 2:9

But we see Jesus, who was made a little lower than the angels for the suffering of death, **crowned with glory and honour**; that he by the grace of God should taste death for every man.

Hebrews 2:10

For it became him, for whom are all things, and by whom are all things, in bringing many sons unto **glory**, to make the captain of their salvation perfect through sufferings.

Hebrews 3:3

For this man was counted worthy of more **glory** than Moses, inasmuch as he who hath builded the house hath more honour than the house.

Hebrews 8:1

Now of the things which we have spoken this is the sum: We have such an high priest, who is set on the right hand of the throne of the **Majesty** in the heavens;

Hebrews 9:5
And over it the cherubims of **glory** shadowing the mercyseat; of which we cannot now speak particularly.

Hebrews 9:24
For Christ is not entered into the holy places made with hands, which are the figures of the true; but into heaven itself, now to appear in the **presence** (Glory) of God for us:

Hebrews 12:28-29
Wherefore we receiving a kingdom which cannot be moved, let us have grace, whereby we may serve God acceptably with reverence and godly fear:

For our God is **a consuming fire (Glory-fire).**
Hebrews 13:21
Make you perfect in every good work to do his will, working in you that which is wellpleasing in his sight, through Jesus Christ; to whom be **glory** for ever and ever. Amen.

The Book of James

James 2:1

My brethren, have not the faith of our Lord Jesus Christ, **the Lord of glory**, with respect of persons.

The Books of 1 & 2 Peter

1 Peter 1:7

That the trial of your faith, being much more precious than of gold that perisheth, though it be tried with fire, might be found unto praise and honour and **glory** at the appearing of Jesus Christ:

1 Peter 1:8

Whom having not seen, ye love; in whom, though now ye see him not, yet believing, ye rejoice with joy unspeakable and **full of glory**:

1 Peter 1:11

Searching what, or what manner of time the Spirit of Christ which was in them did signify, when it testified beforehand the sufferings of Christ, and the **glory** that should follow.

1 Peter 1:21
Who by him do believe in God, that raised him up from the dead, and gave him **glory**; that your faith and hope might be in God.

1 Peter 1:24
For all flesh is as grass, and all the **glory** of man as the flower of grass. The grass withereth, and the flower thereof falleth away:

1 Peter 4:13
But rejoice, inasmuch as ye are partakers of Christ's sufferings; that, when **his glory** shall be revealed, ye may be glad also with exceeding joy.

1 Peter 4:14
If ye be reproached for the name of Christ, happy are ye; for **the Spirit of Glory** and of God resteth upon you: on their part he is evil spoken of, but on your part he is **glorified.**

1 Peter 5:1
The elders which are among you I exhort, who am also an elder, and a witness of the sufferings of Christ, and also a partaker of the **glory** that shall be revealed:

1 Peter 5:4

And when the chief Shepherd shall appear, ye shall receive a crown of **glory** that fadeth not away.

1 Peter 5:10

But the God of all grace, who hath called us unto **his eternal glory** by Christ Jesus, after that ye have suffered a while, make you perfect, stablish, strengthen, settle you.

1 Peter 5:11

To him be **glory** and dominion for ever and ever. Amen.

2 Peter 1:3

According as his divine power hath given unto us all things that pertain unto life and godliness, through the knowledge of him that **hath called us to glory and virtue:**

2 Peter 1:3 - 4

" As His divine power (the Holy Spirit) has given to us all things that pertain to life and godliness, through the knowledge of Him(Christ Jesus) who called us **by Glory and virtue**, by which have been given to us exceedingly great and precious promises (the Word), that through these you may be partakers of the **Divine Nature (the Glory of the Father)…"**

2 Peter 1:16-17
For we have not followed cunningly devised fables, when we made known unto you the power and coming of our Lord Jesus Christ, but were eyewitnesses of his **majesty.** For he received from God the Father honour and **glory,** when there came such a voice to him from the excellent **glory,** This is my beloved Son, in whom I am well pleased.

2 Peter 3:18
But grow in grace, and in the knowledge of our Lord and Saviour Jesus Christ. To him be **glory** both now and for ever. Amen.

The Book of Jude

Jude 1:24-25
Now unto him that is able to keep you from falling, and to present you faultless before the presence of his **glory** with exceeding joy,
To the only wise God our Saviour, be **glory** and majesty, dominion and power, both now and ever. Amen.

The Book of Revelation

Revelation 1:6
And hath made us kings and priests unto God and his Father; to him be **glory** and dominion for ever and ever. Amen.

Revelation 1:14-16
His head and his hairs were white like wool, as white as snow; and his eyes were as a flame of fire ; And his feet like unto fine brass, as if they burned in a furnace; and his voice as the sound of many waters. And he had in his right hand seven stars: and out of his mouth went a sharp twoedged sword: **and his countenance was as the sun shineth in his strength.**

Revelation 2:18
These things saith the Son of God, who hath **his eyes like unto a flame of fire , and his feet are like fine brass;**

Revelation 4:5
And out of the throne proceeded **lightnings and thunderings** and voices: and there were **seven lamps of fire burning** before the throne, which are the seven Spirits of God.

Revelation 4:9
And when those beasts give **glory** and honour and thanks to him that sat on the throne, who liveth for ever and ever,

Revelation 4:11
Thou art worthy, O Lord, to receive **glory** and honour and power: for thou hast created all things, and for thy pleasure they are and were created.

Revelation 5:12
Saying with a loud voice, Worthy is the Lamb that was slain to receive power, and riches, and wisdom, and strength, and honour, and **glory**, and blessing.

Revelation 5:13
And every creature which is in heaven, and on the earth, and under the earth, and such as are in the sea, and all that are in them, heard I saying, Blessing, and honour, and **glory**, and power, be unto him that sitteth upon the throne, and unto the Lamb for ever and ever.

Revelation 7:12
Saying, Amen: Blessing, and **glory**, and wisdom, and thanksgiving, and honour, and power, and

might, be unto our God for ever and ever.
Amen.

Revelation 10:1-3

And I saw another mighty angel come down
from heaven, **clothed with a cloud: and a
rainbow was upon his head, and his face was
as it were the sun, and his feet as pillars of
fire** : And he had in his hand a little book open:
and he set his right foot upon the sea, and his left
foot on the earth, And cried with a loud voice, as
when a lion roareth: and when he had cried,
seven thunders uttered their voices.

Revelation 11:13

And the same hour was there a great earthquake,
and the tenth part of the city fell, and in the
earthquake were slain of men seven thousand:
and the remnant were affrighted, and gave **glory**
to the God of heaven.

Revelation 11:19

And the temple of God was opened in heaven,
and there was seen in his temple the ark of his
testament: **and there were lightnings, and
voices, and thunderings, and an earthquake,
and great hail.**

Revelation 14:7
Saying with a loud voice, Fear God, and give **glory** to him; for the hour of his judgment is come: and worship him that made heaven, and earth, and the sea, and the fountains of waters.

Revelation 15:8
And the temple was filled with smoke from the **glory of God**, and from his power; and no man was able to enter into the temple, till the seven plagues of the seven angels were fulfilled.

Revelation 16:9
And men were scorched with great heat, and blasphemed the name of God, which hath power over these plagues: and they repented not to give him **glory**.

Revelation 18:1
And after these things I saw another angel come down from heaven, having great power; **and the earth was lightened with his glory.**

Revelation 19 :1
And after these things I heard a great voice of much people in heaven, saying, Alleluia; Salvation, and **glory**, and honour, and power, unto the Lord our God:

Revelation 19:11-13
And I saw heaven opened, and behold a white horse; and he that sat upon him was called Faithful and True, and in righteousness he doth judge and make war. **His eyes were as a flame of fire,** and on his head were many crowns; and he had a name written, that no man knew, but he himself. And he was clothed with a vesture dipped in blood: and his name is called The Word of God.

Revelation 21:11
Having **the glory of God**: and her light was like unto a stone most precious, even like a jasper stone, clear as crystal;

Revelation 21:11(Amplified)
Having **God's glory [filled with His radiant light].** The **brilliance** of it resembled a rare *and* very precious jewel, like jasper, shining *and* clear as crystal.

Revelation 21:23
And the city had no need of the sun, neither of the moon, to shine in it: **for the glory of God did lighten it, and the Lamb is the light thereof.**

ABOUT THE AUTHOR

JOHN ECKHARDT is overseer of Crusaders Ministries, located in Chicago, Illinois. Anointed with a strong apostolic grace, he has ministered throughout the United States and overseas in more than eighty nations. He is founder and overseer of the Impact Network, a sought-after international conference speaker, and has authored more than forty books including Prayers That Rout Demons, God Still Speaks and Prophet Arise. He resides in the Chicago area with his wife, Wanda, their five children and son in law.

FOR MORE INFORMATION

www.johneckhardtministries.com